MW01251321

Landforms

by Lynn Van Gorp

Science Contributor
Sally Ride Science
Science Consultants
William B. Rice, Geologist
Nancy McKeown, Geologist

First hardcover edition published in 2009 by
Compass Point Books
151 Good Counsel Drive
P.O. Box 669
Mankato, MN 56002-0669

Editor: Mari Bolte
Designer: Heidi Thompson
Editorial Contributor: Sue Vander Hook

Art Director: LuAnn Ascheman-Adams
Creative Director: Joe Ewest
Editorial Director: Nick Healy
Managing Editor: Catherine Neitge
Cartographer: XNR Productions, Inc.
Illustrator: Eric Hoffman

 This book was manufactured with paper containing at least 10 percent post-consumer waste.

Library of Congress Cataloging-in-Publication Data
Van Gorp, Lynn.
  Landforms / by Lynn Van Gorp.
    p. cm.—(Mission: science)
  Includes index.
  ISBN 978-0-7565-4234-4 (library binding)
  1. Landforms—Juvenile literature. I. Title. II. Series.
  GB406.V36 2010
  551.41—dc22   2009002819

Visit Compass Point Books on the Internet at *www.compasspointbooks.com*
or e-mail your request to *custserv@compasspointbooks.com*

Table of Contents

Unique Landforms

Imagine yourself on a hike with your friends. You are surrounded by mountains, and ahead is an outcropping of rocks. It seems as if a giant hand reached out and stuck the rocks into the side of the mountain. When you walk a little farther, you see a wide, green valley. How did this all come to be?

What you saw on your imaginary hike were unique landforms—a variety of shapes and features that make up the surface of Earth. Landforms are sculpted by the natural processes of an ever-changing planet.

Scientists study landforms to learn about how Earth has changed in the past. That knowledge can also help them predict what changes might take place in the future.

Two types of forces change Earth's surface: constructive forces and destructive forces. Constructive forces such as earthquakes and volcanoes build up the surface of Earth. Destructive forces such as weathering and erosion wear it down.

Did You Know?

The study of landforms is called geomorphology. It is the part of science that studies the changes in Earth's surface. It also examines the forces and processes that create them.

◀ Many landforms are well-known for their distinctive shapes, sizes, and colors. Bryce Canyon in Utah is known for its red rock spires and amphitheaters caused by erosion.

Types of Landforms

Mountains, plains, and plateaus are types of landforms. A mountain is naturally elevated above the surface of Earth, usually with steep sides and towering peaks. Mount Everest is the highest mountain on Earth, towering 29,029 feet (8,848 meters) above sea level. A plain is a landform with flat or gently rolling land and usually has no trees. Plains have low relief, a small difference between the highest and lowest parts of the landform. Plateaus have high elevation but are level on top, sort of like a table. Other types of landforms include mesas, swamps, savannas, canyons, and reefs.

Mapping Earth's Surface

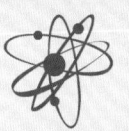

People use road maps to figure out where they are going and how to get there. But there are many other types of maps, including topographic, climate, and physical.

Topographic maps show the shape and elevation of an area. Contour lines indicate natural and man-made features.

Climate maps give information regarding the climate and environment in an area. They use various colors to represent temperatures or precipitation levels.

Physical maps show the physical features of an area, such as mountains, lakes, and rivers, through illustration. For example, lakes and rivers would

The contour lines of topographic maps show height and depth in the landscape.

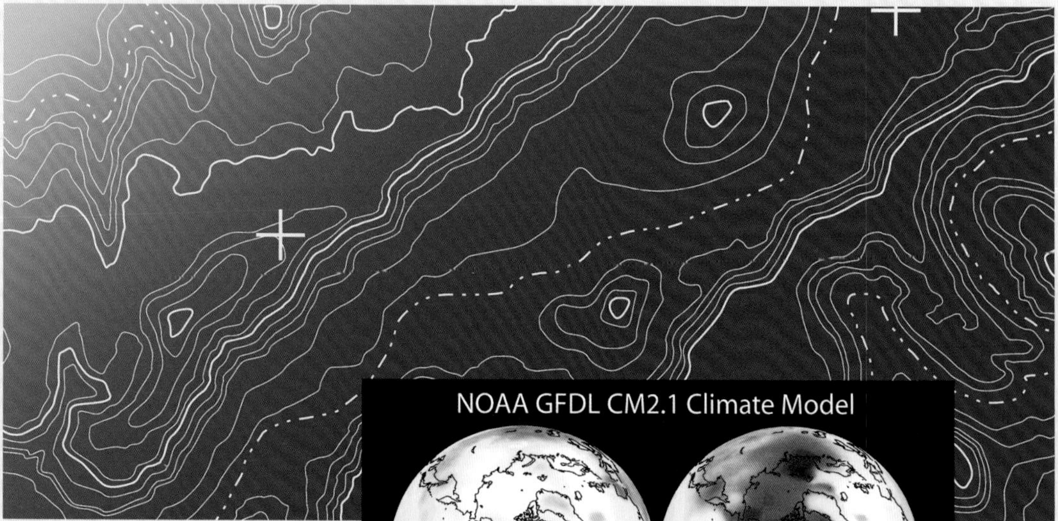

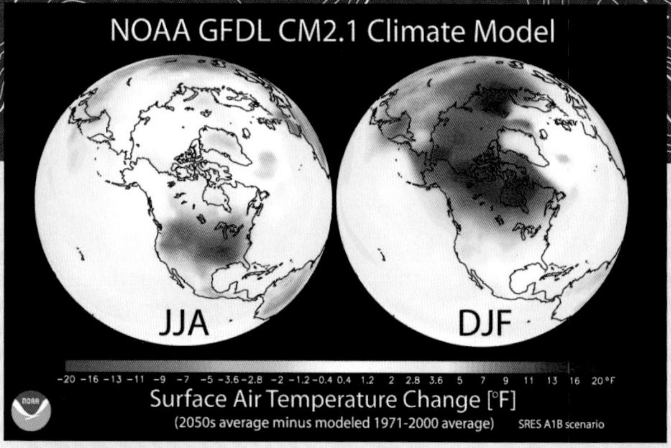
NOAA GFDL CM2.1 Climate Model
JJA
DJF
-20 -16 -13 -11 -9 -7 -5 -3.6 -2.8 -2 -1.2 -0.4 0.4 1.2 2 2.8 3.6 5 7 9 11 13 16 20°F
Surface Air Temperature Change [°F]
(2050s average minus modeled 1971-2000 average)
SRES A1B scenario

Climate maps help scientists monitor changes in Earth's climate, such as global warming.

be shown in blue, while elevations would be "earth" colors, with lower elevations shown in green and higher elevations in brown.

Other types of physical maps show where people live, where they can travel, and how the land is used.

Physical maps are easy to use.

For hundreds of years, mapmakers—called cartographers—drew or painted maps by hand. Often they were explorers who made maps from what they saw or what other people told them. It took a long time to draw maps, and no one knew how correct they were. The development of instruments such as the compass and telescope helped cartographers make more accurate maps.

Over the years, mapmaking has changed a great deal. Aerial photography became

New Orleans, Louisiana, August 24, 2002, before Hurricane Katrina

New Orleans, Louisiana, September 2, 2005, after Hurricane Katrina

Imaging Earth

The greatest change in mapmaking came in 1972, when the *Landsat 1* satellite was launched into space. The satellite was equipped with a scanner designed to take photographs of Earth and transmit them back. Computers on the ground used the information to make extremely accurate maps.

Landsat 1 also recorded the effects of storms and earthquakes.

During its six years of service, *Landsat 1* took more than 300,000 images of Earth's surface. Six more Landsat satellites followed the original, with the launch of the *Landsat 7* satellite in 1999.

Mapping the Northwest

The Lewis and Clark expedition, headed by Meriwether Lewis and William Clark, mapped previously uncharted territory in the Northwest. The explorers traveled nearly 7,700 miles (12,397 kilometers) and recorded the presence of 178 plants and 122 animals for the first time.

Clark began creating his maps at the beginning of the expedition in 1804. He continued during the journey and after. His maps inspired groups of settlers and other explorers to move west.

Lewis and Clark's expedition started in Missouri and traveled through the future states of Kansas, Nebraska, Iowa, South Dakota, North Dakota, Montana, Idaho, Washington, and Oregon.

the basis for mapmaking, especially topographic maps. Cartographers could more accurately map areas of land or sea by using pictures taken by airplanes or satellites. The use of computers transformed cartography almost into a science, with complex software programs that can quickly create detailed, accurate maps.

An earthquake, volcano, or other natural disaster can quickly change the terrain and alter landforms. People in certain parts of the world are very familiar with earthquakes. They are accustomed to the shaking and rolling that occur when large slabs of Earth's crust, called tectonic plates, shift and crash into each other. When plates move and shift, the surface of Earth may tremble for hundreds of miles around. In just a few seconds, an earthquake can change the topography of the land.

The outer shell of Earth's crust is not one big piece. There are 14 large tectonic plates, as well as a number of smaller plates—large pieces of crust that float on liquid magma underneath. When the edges of two plates scrape or collide, stress builds up on one section of the crust. The stressed area is called a fault. During an earthquake, there is movement at the fault line—movement that can change or create landforms.

Types of Faults

Earth's crust has three main types of faults: normal, reverse, and strike-slip. Faults are classified by how the plates on either side of the fault move in relation to each other. A normal fault occurs when one plate drops lower than the other plate. The Rio Grande Valley in New Mexico is an example of a landform created by a normal fault.

Did You Know?

Although it is impossible to predict exactly when an earthquake will occur, scientists can use data to predict where future earthquakes may strike.

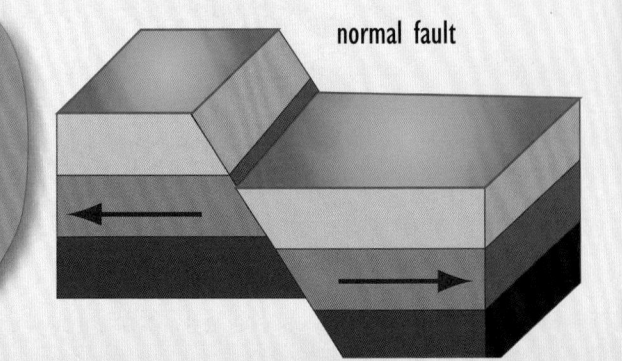

normal fault

Along a reverse fault, one plate is pushed up and over the other plate. The plates overlap at an angle. Stress from an earthquake pushes the two plates closer together, and the upper plate overlaps the other plate even more. Evidence of a reverse fault can be found at Glacier National Park in Montana.

The third kind of fault, a strike-slip fault, occurs when two plates are at the same horizontal level. Sometimes they slide past each other and scrape. Instead of the up-and-down movement of the other faults, the plates at a strike-slip fault graze each other as they pass by. The San Andreas Fault in California is an example of a strike-slip fault.

reverse fault

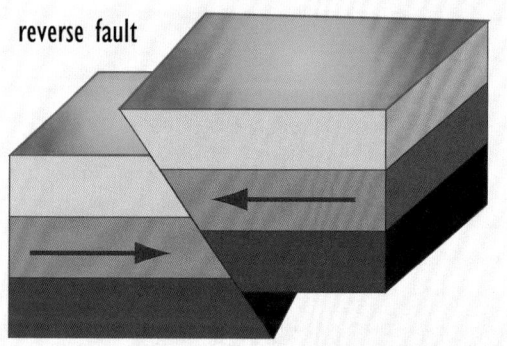

strike-slip fault

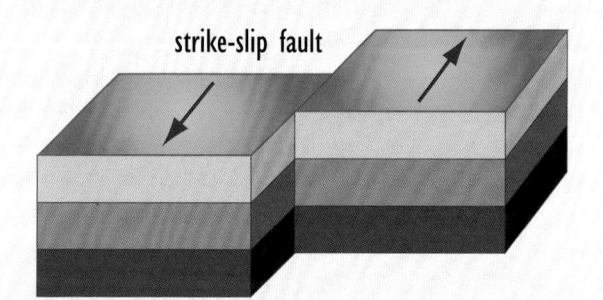

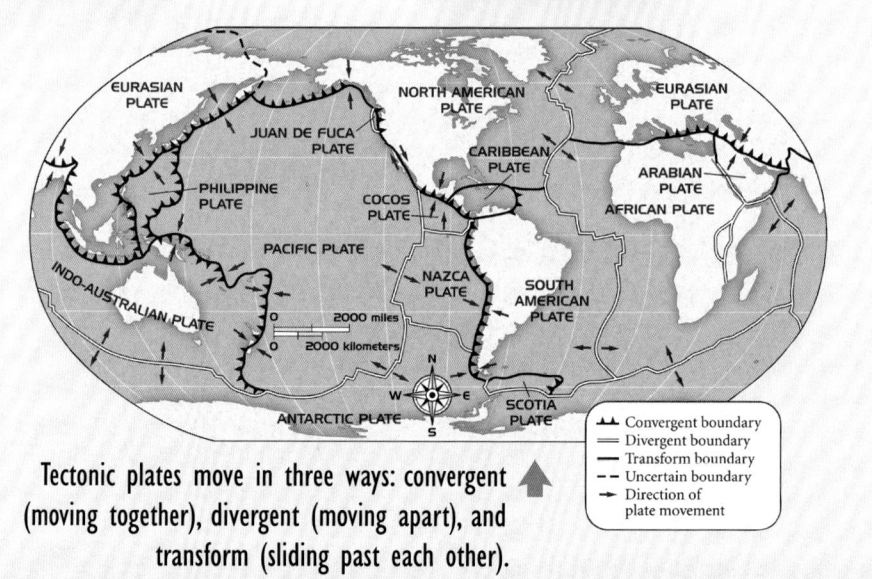

Tectonic plates move in three ways: convergent (moving together), divergent (moving apart), and transform (sliding past each other).

Volcanoes

Volcanoes usually form where tectonic plates collide or spread apart. More than half of all active volcanoes exist along the edge of the Pacific plate, a place known as the Ring of Fire.

Indonesia, Japan, and the United States have the most active volcanoes. Volcanoes have created some of the most beautiful landforms on Earth. The Hawaiian Islands and Mount Fuji in Japan were both formed by volcanoes, but they look very different. The Hawaiian Islands were formed by trails of flowing lava that spread out to create a flat but rough landscape. Mount Fuji, on the other hand, is the result of numerous explosive eruptions that formed a tall, cone-shaped mountain.

Volcanoes that erupt can create trails of death and destruction. Mount Etna in Italy, one of the most active volcanoes in the world, is almost constantly erupting. The explosive eruption of 1928 sent lava flowing into the town of Mascali, destroying it in just two days. Mount Etna erupted 16 times from January through July 2001. On July 13, an

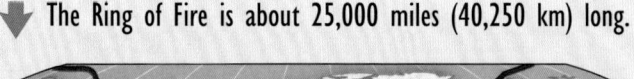

The Ring of Fire is about 25,000 miles (40,250 km) long.

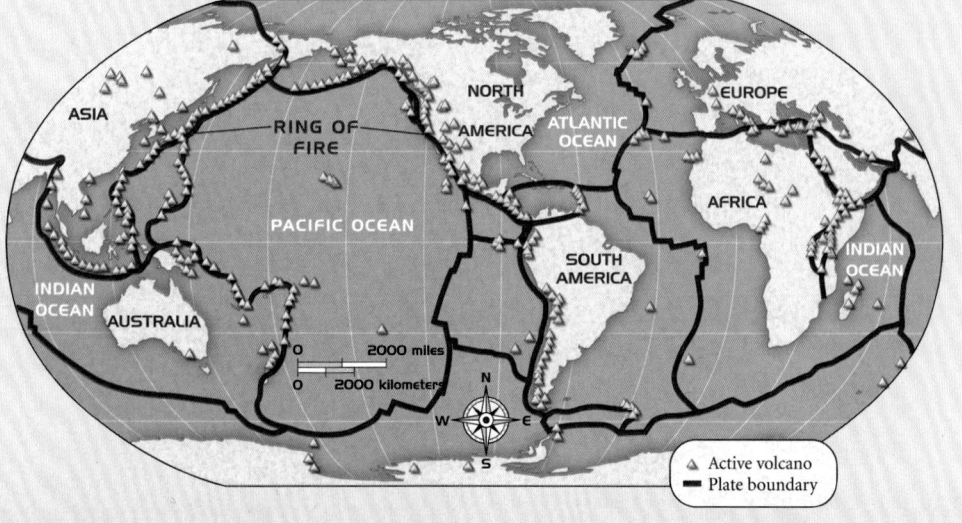

especially large eruption released large quantities of steam, smoke, and lava. The lava flow came within 3 miles (4.8 km) of a nearby town. An eruption in 2002 created a cloud of ash that traveled more than 350 miles (564 km) across the Mediterranean Sea.

In March 1980, Mount St. Helens in Washington erupted, causing the most deadly and expensive volcanic eruption ever in the United States. The eruption was followed by two months of earthquakes and periods of steam venting. Winds blew 520 million tons (473 metric tons) of volcanic ash across the United States. The heavy ash caused almost complete darkness in Spokane, Washington, nearly 250 miles (403 km)

east of Mount St. Helens. Fifty-seven people, 7,000 large animals, and 12 million hatchery salmon were killed as a result. Five more eruptions occurred that year.

Mountain Fun

Have you ever thought about climbing a mountain? You don't need to start with Mount Everest. You can begin with easy hikes near your home.

The difficulty of a climb is based on two factors: altitude and terrain. The easiest mountains to climb are usually volcanoes, which tend to have easier paths to the top and can be completed in one or two days. Diamond Head in Hawaii is a popular climbing destination. Its 0.7 mile (1.1 km) climb takes about an hour to complete. The most difficult mountains include Mount Everest and K2 in central Asia. These mountains reach heights of more than 28,000 feet (8,500 meters) and are suited for professional climbers only.

Did You Know?

There are more than 600 active volcanoes on land. There are many more on the seafloor. Between 50 and 70 volcanoes erupt every year.

Types of Eruptions

Volcanoes erupt in a variety of ways. A quiet eruption occurs if the lava is thin and flows easily. Iceland was formed from quiet eruptions over time, which released two types of lava—fast-moving, very hot lava, which hardens into a rippled surface, cooler, slower-moving lava hardens into rough chunks.

An explosive eruption occurs if the lava is thick and sticky. Since it's too thick to flow out quietly, it builds up inside Earth until it explodes. The blast scatters lava called tephra into pieces, some as small as ash and others as large as a car or a house. The eruption of Mount St. Helens in 1980 was explosive.

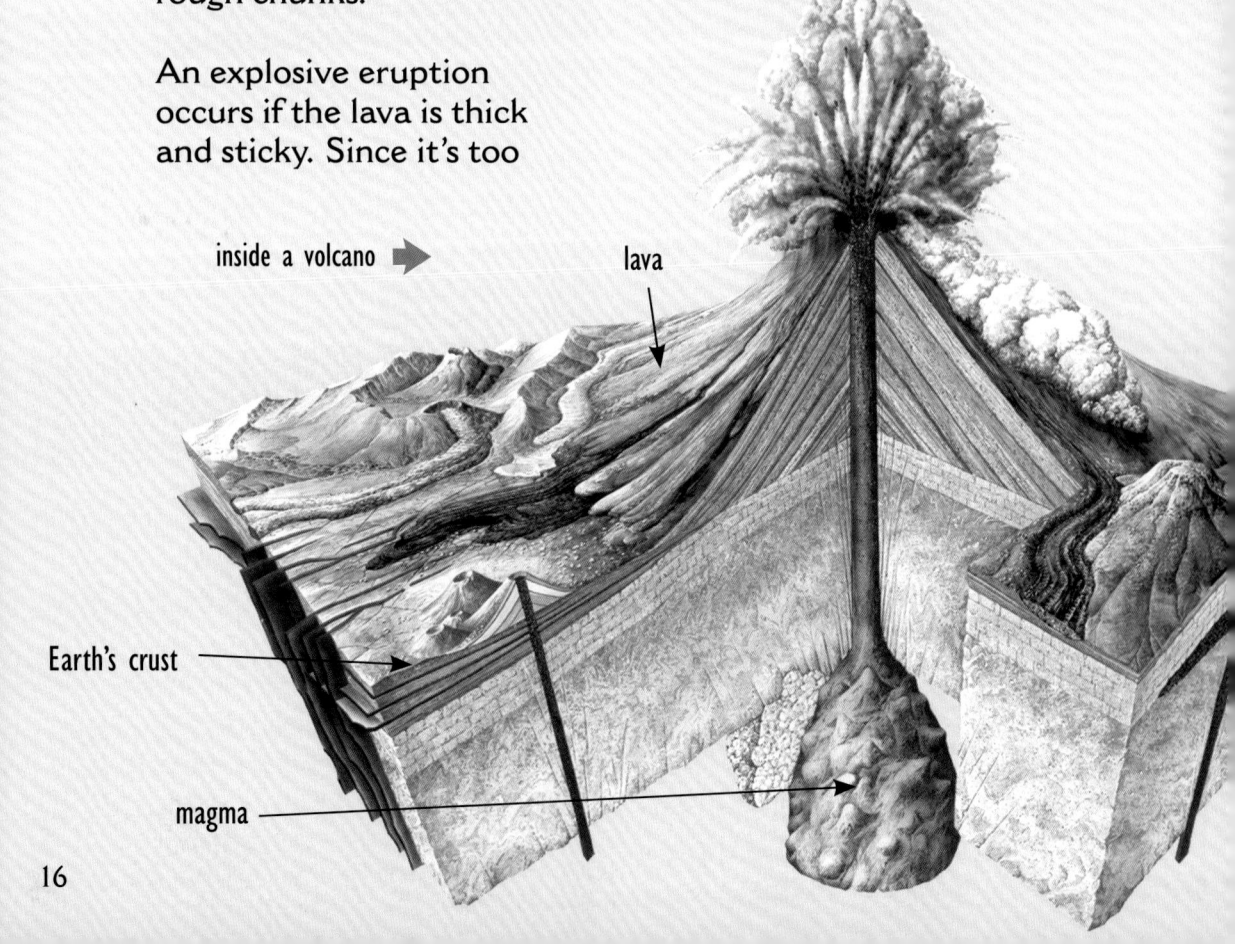

inside a volcano ➡

lava

Earth's crust

magma

Some volcanoes come from hot spots far underground. A hot spot is an area where magma melts through the crust like a blowtorch. It happens where a plate is solid, not where it intersects with another plate. The Hawaiian Islands were formed from eruptions caused by a hot spot on the ocean floor. Hot spots underneath Yellowstone National Park produce remarkable geysers, hot springs, and bubbling mud.

Sometimes magma doesn't reach the surface of Earth. It hardens underneath other rock or inside a volcanic mountain. It can't be seen until the outer rock wears away. Shiprock in New Mexico is an example of magma that hardened inside a volcano. When the rock around it wore away, a huge formation remained, towering 1,700 feet (518 m) above the ground.

Did You Know?

Molten lava reaches temperatures ranging from 1,382 to 2,282 degrees Fahrenheit (750 and 1,250 degrees Celsius).

Mount St. Helens, Washington

Shiprock, New Mexico

Weathering

Landforms change with earthquakes and volcanoes, but they also change from natural weathering. It takes place when rocks are broken or worn down into smaller pieces by the weather. This happens slowly, but weathering can eventually wear down entire mountains. There are two types of weathering: natural and chemical. Natural weathering occurs through natural processes that cause rocks to crack, crumble, and flake. For example, when water freezes in a crack in a rock, it expands. This widens the crack and weakens the rock. Rocks can also be worn down when they no

Fox Glacier in New Zealand is constantly expanding and contracting. The heavy sheets of ice break off rock and carry the pieces down the mountain.

longer have ground cover and are not protected. Wind and water can carry sand and other material across the surface of bare rock, scratching it and wearing it down.

Chemical weathering happens when chemicals in the water and air form holes and soft spots in rocks. The rocks will eventually fall apart. Carbon dioxide in water creates an acid that weakens marble and limestone. Plants also make a weak acid that slowly dissolves the rock around them.

Sometimes chemical damage is man-made. Burning coal, oil, and gas can pollute the air. Eventually rainwater transports acid from the pollution back down to the earth. The result is acid rain, which eats away at whatever it touches.

Quick Damage

Acid rain is the most destructive form of chemical weathering. It causes quick changes to landforms and wears down buildings and statues exposed to the rain. Areas on the East Coast, such as New York and Washington, D.C., receive rainfall that has 10 times the amount of acid as regular rain. Some national monuments, which were built to last for thousands of years, have been heavily damaged in as little as one or two decades. The Grant Memorial in Washington, D.C., built in 1922, is a good example of this. Acid rain has turned the bronze sculptures and the marble bases green.

Have you ever made a sand castle? What happened when a wave swept it away? Your ruined sand castle is an example of erosion. A variety of forces cause erosion, including water, wind, ice, mud, waves, and wind. Erosion is the movement of soil, mud, rock, and other particles away from an area of land. The materials that move are called sediment.

Gravity also causes erosion. It is the force that pulls sediment downhill. Landslides happen when rocks and soil move suddenly down a hillside. They often occur when part of a hillside has been cut away for roads or houses.

Mudflows, also known as mudslides, are the rapid movement of mud down a hillside. Mud is a mixture of rock, soil, and water. Mudflows often occur after a heavy rainfall in a normally dry area.

A slump occurs when a large piece of land moves a short distance down all at once. The land is loosened, sometimes from draining water that creates a path under a section of rock and soil. The water flow weakens the soil's hold on the slope. When the soil can no longer hold on, it suddenly gives way and slips down the hillside.

Mudflows are the fastest form of erosion, moving at speeds from 10 to 35 miles (16 to 56 km) per hour.

Taking a Mud Bath

Mud volcanoes occur when gas deposits put pressure on mud and sand under Earth's surface. Eventually the deposits reach the surface and cause eruptions. Mud volcanoes are usually found along fault lines and are one of the indicators of oil and gas reserves. They are usually small and harmless.

In May 2006, a mud volcano erupted near Surabaya, Indonesia's second largest city. About 3.5 million cubic feet (100,000 cubic meters) of mud flows from the volcano every day—enough to fill more than 50 Olympic-sized pools.

Attempts to stop the mudflow have included the building of dams and levees, creating channels into the sea, and plugging the crater with concrete balls. So far all attempts have failed.

The mud is causing the land to sink at a rate of nearly 40 feet (12.2 m) a year. More than 60,000 people have fled their homes. The volcano, which officials believe was caused by a drilling accident, has become one of the largest mud volcanoes to hit a populated area. Experts predict that the mudflow could go on for years or even decades.

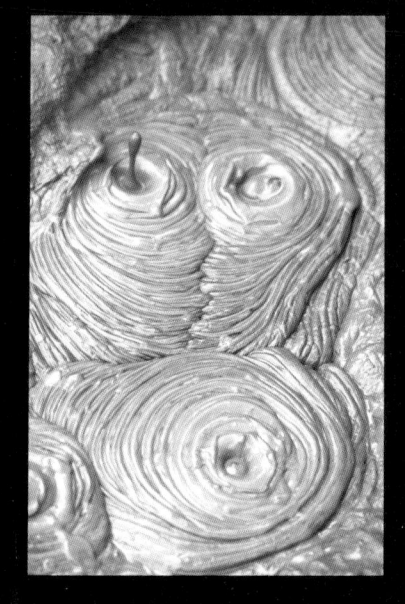

Glaciers

A glacier is a large mass of ice and snow that moves slowly over land. As it moves, it changes the landscape. Gravity causes some glaciers to move down hills or mountains.

There are two main types of glaciers: valley glaciers and continental glaciers. Valley glaciers are long, narrow buildups of snow and ice that form in mountain terrain. Continental glaciers, also called ice sheets, can cover large areas of land. During the peak of the last glacial period, about 20,000 years ago, large glaciers covered parts of North America, Europe, and Asia. Today glaciers cover Antarctica and most of Greenland. The World Glacier Inventory at the University of Colorado has recorded the locations of more than 100,000 glaciers.

When a glacier moves, its sheer weight breaks apart rock. Some of the rocks are small, but others are boulders as large as a house. The broken rocks and soil freeze to the bottom of the glacier. When the glacier moves again, the rocks and soil move with it, scratching and gouging the earth below. When a glacier melts, it deposits the material it accumulated in its path, creating a new landform.

Geologists believe that the Great Lakes along the U.S.-Canadian border were formed when a huge ice sheet melted about 10,000 years ago. When the glacier melted, the water filled up the large basins carved out by the shifting glacier.

Did You Know?

The Great Lakes—Superior, Michigan, Huron, Erie, and Ontario—make up the largest group of freshwater lakes on Earth.

Glaciers: Not Just Old Ice

The glaciers in the Canadian Rocky Mountains make up just a small part of the thick ice mass that once covered western Canada's mountains. During the past 2 million years, layers of hard-packed snow were formed into a 990-foot (300-m) thick layer of glacial ice.

The glaciers hold many secrets to the past— more than 100,000 fossils have been found within the glacier's many layers.

Global warming is having an impact on the glaciers. In 2007 scientists found exposed tree stumps that had been covered for the past 7,000 years. Scientists estimate that some of the Canadian glaciers have lost as much as 70 percent of their volume over the past century.

Flowing Water

Have you ever poured water over a pile of sand? It doesn't take much water for the sand to crumble and spread out. Think about what a river or stream can do. Flowing water alters Earth's surface more than any other form of erosion.

As water moves faster, it picks up and carries larger objects. Water picks up anything in its path—silt, sand, rocks, twigs, fossils—and eventually deposits them somewhere else. Along the way, water changes landforms. Trees and other ground cover can slow down the erosion process by holding back some of the water and keeping the soil and rock in place.

When heavy rains cause a river or lake to overflow, the surrounding area floods. When the water recedes, it leaves behind sediment. Some sediment is rich soil that is ideal for growing crops.

Overflowing water can also create a waterfall. Waterfalls form when water passes over rock that is hard enough to resist erosion. Niagara Falls on the New York-Ontario border formed because the top layer of rock was harder than the layer below it. The river washed away the soft rock more quickly than the layer on top. Pieces of the hard top layer broke away, creating the waterfall's sharp edge and steep drop.

Over the Edge

The tallest waterfall in the world is Angel Falls in Venezuela. It is 3,212 feet (979 m) high. The water drops more than twice the height of the Empire State Building and 15 times that of Niagara Falls.

Walking on an extremely windy day can be treacherous. The wind can push you from side to side or sometimes keep you from moving forward. A strong enough gust can knock you right off your feet.

Wind can cause a lot of damage. It also causes landforms to change. Wind is especially destructive in deserts, where the land has few plants to hold the sand in place. Winds blow across the desert, picking up the smallest particles and carrying them until they fall. Swift winds carry more substances with them, lifting the lighter materials higher and moving them faster than the heavier substances.

During the 1930s, strong winds blew away tons of topsoil from U.S. farmlands. Dust storms happened regularly in a time that came to be called the Dust Bowl. Plowing up too much of the land let the wind destroy the trees and prairie grass that had once protected the soil from erosion.

Super Sand Dunes

The tallest sand dunes in the world are in the huge Namib Desert in Namibia. Some dunes peak at nearly 1,000 feet (300 m).

Considered to be one of the oldest deserts, it stretches more than 1,200 miles (1,920 km) long but averages only 70 miles (112 km) wide. The Namib Desert is so dry that it receives more moisture from ocean fog than from annual rainfall.

A satellite view of the Namib Desert ➡ along the Atlantic coast of Africa

When wind is stopped by something like a tree, plant, or hill, it drops what it is carrying. Sometimes the sand that falls forms a sand dune. Dunes are common in the desert and along coastal areas. People visit areas covered by massive sand dunes to enjoy the landscape, but also to ride dune buggies on the mounds and valleys shaped by the shifting sand.

Did You Know?

During 1933 and 1934, more than 100 million acres (39 million hectares) of topsoil was blown away in the Dust Bowl area of the midwestern and southern plains. This led to the worst drought in U.S. history. Twenty-seven states were affected by the drought.

The Dust Bowl lasted from 1931 to 1939.

Waves

Ocean waves are constantly changing the landscape of coastlines and beaches. They erode the shore in some places and build it up in others.

Wind is one source of energy for waves. It blows across the water's surface, causing the water to move up and down. When the force of a wave hits shore, it breaks rocks into small pieces and carries sand to new locations or drags it back into the sea. The continued force of waves can form cliffs and caves on the shoreline. A combination of water and salt can also erode a rocky coastline.

Many communities try to protect their shores from erosion. People sometimes fill sandbags and stack them along the most exposed beaches to hold back the water and protect their sandy beaches. Some waves, however, are so huge that residents can only attempt to protect themselves and escape the area. These waves are called tsunamis.

Underwater Diving

The floor of the ocean holds remarkable landforms. Most of them were formed by earthquakes and volcanoes that ooze magma at tectonic plate boundaries. Basins formed by these phenomena are ideal environments for coral reefs, structures shaped by the deposits of living organisms.

Australia's Great Barrier Reef, with about 900 islands and nearly 3,000 reefs, is the largest coral reef system in the world. The area is home to thousands of fish, sea snakes, sea turtles, whales, dolphins, and porpoises.

Did You Know?

Tsunami is a Japanese word meaning harbor wave.

Tsunamis form in the ocean when an underwater earthquake or volcanic eruption forcefully pushes a huge amount of water to the surface. When a tsunami arrives at the shallow waters of a coastline, it rises to an enormous height and crashes down on shore. Its massive force can alter and displace hundreds of miles of coastland.

More than 1.5 million people were left homeless by the December 2004 tsunami.

Monster Waves

On December 26, 2004, tsunamis hit 11 countries on the Indian Ocean including Thailand, Indonesia, Burma (Myanmar), and Malaysia. More than 225,000 people were killed. Some tsunamis rose as high as 100 feet (30 m), creating one of the deadliest natural disasters in history. Scientists have since tried to retrace the path of the waves to learn how and why the water moved in the directions it did. The more they learn, the more prepared people can be when another tsunami hits.

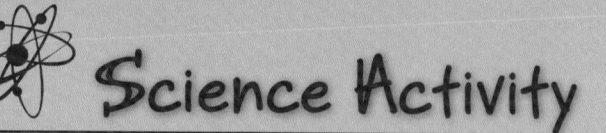
Earth Movement

In this science activity, you will explore the effects of rainfall on the movement of earth down a slope.

Materials

- soil
- sand
- gravel
- large tray with edges
- water
- watering can

Procedure

1 Build a model mountain on the large tray with a mixture of gravel, sand, and soil.

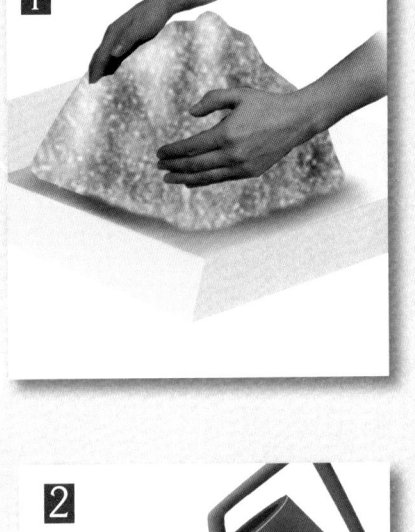

2 Fill the watering can with water; sprinkle water on the mountain to imitate rain.

3 Increase the water flow on the mountain to a pour. What is happening to your mountain now?

4 Record what you see. What type of movement took place? How was the movement different when you changed the flow of water?

5 What type of force is responsible for this type of movement?

Further Study

- Create various landforms, such as hills, valleys, and plains.

- Test the effects of forces such as wind, waves, and flooding.

Important People in Geology

Florence Bascom (1862–1945)
American geologist and one of the first female geologists; studied mountains and how they are formed

William Morris Davis (1850–1934)
American who is considered the founder of American geography and the founder of geomorphology, the study of landforms; described and named the cycle of erosion

William Maurice Ewing (1913–1974)
American oceanographer who made detailed maps of the sea bottom using refraction of waves caused by explosions (similar to sonar); helped describe the Mid-Atlantic Ridge, a long mountain chain running through the Arctic and Atlantic oceans

Grove Harl Gilbert (1843–1918)
Joined a group of 126 scientists who traveled along the coast of Alaska to study glaciers and landforms; took photographs and wrote a book about his studies

Beno Gutenberg (1889–1960)
German-American geologist who determined the boundary between Earth's mantle and core, based on the behavior of earthquake waves

Harry Hammond Hess (1906–1969)
American geologist who developed the theory of seafloor spreading, in which new crust develops at mid-ocean ridges and is destroyed at deep sea trenches

James Hutton (1726–1797)
Scottish farmer who is considered the founder of modern geology; was the first to propose the idea that all geologic features can be explained by rocks from the past; his book *Theory of the Earth* became the basis for modern geology

Charles Lyell (1797–1875)
Scottish geologist who wrote *Principles of Geology*, one of the most influential works on geology; held that fossils were the best guides for describing geologic rock layers

John Milne (1850–1913)
British seismologist and geologist who, in 1880, invented the modern seismograph for measuring earthquake waves

James Wesley Powell (1834–1902)
American geologist who explored the Colorado River through the Grand Canyon and mapped the area; his trip confirmed his theory that erosion from the river had formed the canyon; helped set up the United States Geological Survey in 1879

Charles Francis Richter (1900–1985)
American seismologist who developed a scale for measuring the intensity of earthquakes, called the Richter scale

Joann Stock (1959–)
American professor of geology and geophysics who studies earthquakes that occur on the ocean floor

Alfred Wegener (1880–1930)
German geologist who suggested the idea of the continental drift—that the coastlines of several continents would fit roughly together into a supercontinent; paved the way for the theory of plate tectonics

1086	The *Dream Pool Essays* by Chinese scientist and statesman Shen Kua describe the principles of erosion, uplift, and sedimentation—the foundations of earth science
1546	German physician and scientist Georgius Agricola introduces the word *fossil*
1743	British physician and scientist Christopher Packe makes a geological map of the southeast portion of England
1760	British geologist and astronomer John Michell proposes that earthquakes are caused by one rock layer rubbing against another
1774	German geologist Abraham Werner introduces a classification of minerals
1785	James Hutton presents his study, *Theory of the Earth*, in which he suggests that Earth is very old
1809	William Maclure, called the father of American geology, completes the first geological survey of the eastern United States
1812	German geologist and minerologist Friedrich Mohs creates the Mohs scale to measure the hardness of minerals
1815	English geologist William Smith creates the first large-scale geological map of England and Wales
1830	Charles Lyell publishes *Principles of Geology*, in which he states that the world is several hundred million years old

1903	English astronomer George Darwin and Irish physicist John Joly realize that radioactivity is partly responsible for Earth's heat
1911	British geologist Arthur Holmes uses radioactivity to date rocks
1912	Alfred Wegener puts forward the continental drift theory—that the continents were once joined as a single landmass
1935	Charles Richter develops the Richter scale
1953	American geologists Bruce Heezen and Marie Tharp map the Mid-Atlantic Ridge
1977	Deep-sea vents are discovered around the Galapagos Islands
1990	Oldest portion of the Pacific plate is found
2007	American geologist Vicki Hansen hypothesizes that early meteorites created the first rifts in Earth's crust
2009	Geologists report that an ongoing Indonesian mud volcano also spewed oil for more than a week in March, adding to the already severe environmental damage

Glossary

acid rain—rain, snow, or fog that contains acids made when pollutants mix with water in the air

constructive forces—forces such as earthquakes and volcanoes that build up Earth's surface

crust—Earth's thin outer layer of rock

destructive forces—forces such as weathering and erosion that wear down Earth's surface

earthquake—sudden movement of Earth's crust caused by the release of stress along tectonic plate boundaries

elevation—height above sea level or Earth's surface

erosion—wearing away of rock or soil by wind, water, or ice

erupt—to burst or ooze onto Earth's surface

fault—breaks in the rock of Earth's crust

geomorphology—study of landforms and the forces and processes that form them

glacier—large mass of slowly moving ice

global warming—rise in the average worldwide temperature

gravity—force of attraction between two objects

landforms—natural formations on Earth's surface, such as plains, plateaus, valleys, and mountains

landslide—rapid downward movement of earth, rock, or other debris

lava—magma that reaches Earth's surface and erupts from a volcano

magma—hot, molten rock beneath Earth's crust

mudflow—rapid downward flow of mud

plain—landform with flat or gently rolling land with low relief

plateau—landform with high elevation and a level surface

pollution—introduction of contaminants into an environment

relief—variation in elevation of an area on Earth's surface

runoff—water moving across the surface of Earth, as opposed to soaking into the ground

sediment—sand, mud, and other particles produced from weathering

slope—area of ground where one end is higher than the other

tectonic plates—gigantic slabs of Earth's crust that move around on magma

tephra—volcanic rocks, dust, and ash

terrain—physical features of land

topographic map—map showing the surface features of an area by displaying differences in elevation

tsunami—gigantic ocean wave created by an undersea earthquake, landslide, or volcanic eruption

volcano—vent in Earth's crust from which lava pours; mountain formed from the buildup of lava

wave—raised swell of water that moves across the surface of a large body of water

weathering—breaking down of solid rock into smaller and smaller pieces by wind, water, glaciers, or plant roots

Fradin, Dennis, and Judy Fradin. *Witness to Disaster: Earthquakes.* Washington, D.C.: National Geographic Children's Books, 2008.

Kalman, Bobbie. *Introducing Landforms.* New York: Crabtree Pub., 2008.

Rice, William B. *Rocks and Minerals.* Mankato, Minn.: Compass Point Books, 2009.

Rubin, Ken. *Volcanoes & Earthquakes.* New York: Simon & Schuster Children's Publishing, 2007.

Stille, Darlene. *Plate Tectonics: Earth's Moving Crust.* Minneapolis: Compass Point Books, 2007.

Yep, Laurence. *The Earth Dragon Awakes: The San Francisco Earthquake of 1906.* New York: HarperCollins, 2008.

Internet Sites

FactHound offers a safe, fun way to find Internet sites related to this book. All of the sites on FactHound have been researched by our staff.

Here's all you do:

Visit *www.facthound.com*

FactHound will fetch the best sites for you!

Index

Lynn Van Gorp

Lynn Van Gorp graduated with a master of science degree from the University of Calgary, Canada, and did additional graduate work at the University of Washington, Seattle, and the University of California, Irvine. She has taught for more than 30 years at the elementary and middle school levels and at the university level. Her educational focus areas include science, reading, and technology. She has written a number of student- and teacher-based curriculum-related publications.

Image Credits

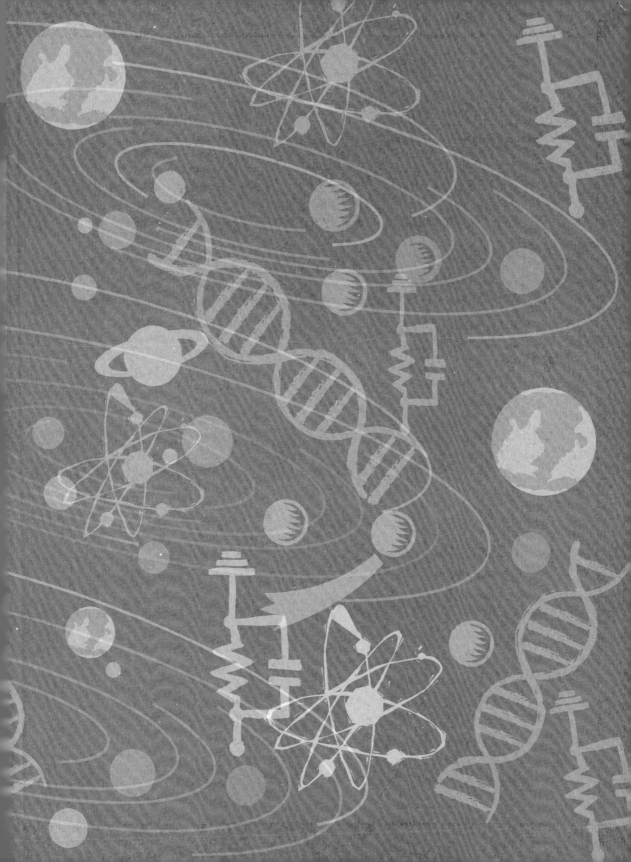